Tori's Adventures
Volume
The Eye Doctor

The day I got my glasses

Story and Photography by
Georgia M. Villalobos

Edited by
John G. Hargrove II

No part of this publication may be reproduced in whole or in part, or stored in a retrieval system, or transmitted in any form or by any means, electronic, mechanical, photocopying, recording, or otherwise, without written permission of the publisher. For information regarding permission, write to:

Georgia M. Villalobos
909 Armory Rd., PMB 111
Barstow, CA 92311

ISBN: 1456318683
EAN-13: 9781456318680

Copyright © 2010 by Georgia M. Villalobos.
All rights reserved. Published by Georgia M. Villalobos

Printed in the U.S.A.

This book is dedicated to my daughter Victoria Joanna Cecilia Villalobos who happens to be blessed with an extra chromosome. Without her, I would have never known the beauty and love that all human beings possess.

Victoria, also known as "Tori" has put us on all kinds of adventures, so we thought we would put them into stories, we call them "Tori's Adventures." And so the stories begin.

A special thanks to Dr. Richard Kennedy for allowing us to use him, his staff and his facility in our book.

My mommy said I should have my eyes checked because my mommy and my sister just got their eyes checked and they need glasses.

So, today I had my eyes checked for the first time.

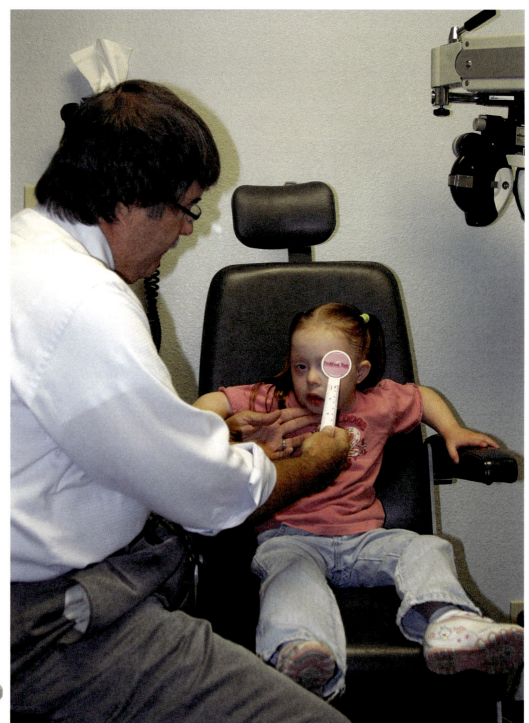

The doctor used this stick with stickers on it to cover one eye to make me look with the other eye.

My mom says the stick is called a *Fixation Stick*.

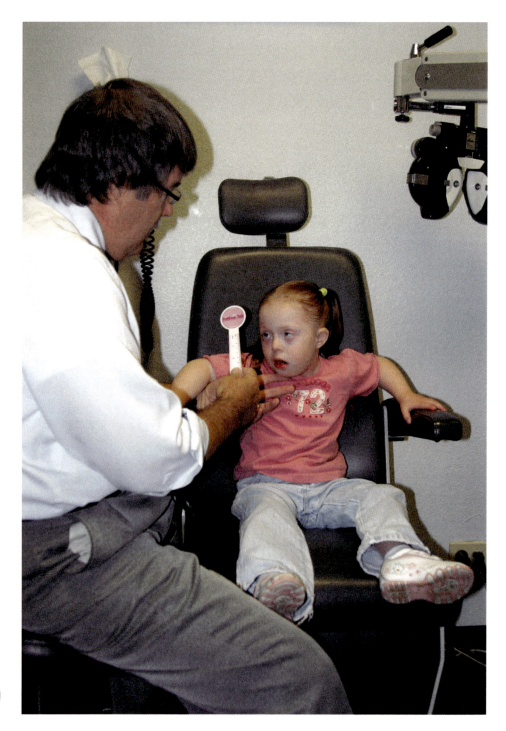

The doctor also used the funny stick to make me look at it when he moved it back and forth in front of me.

My mommy said it was for "following" my eyes. It was to see if I can follow the stick with my eyes the way I am supposed to do.

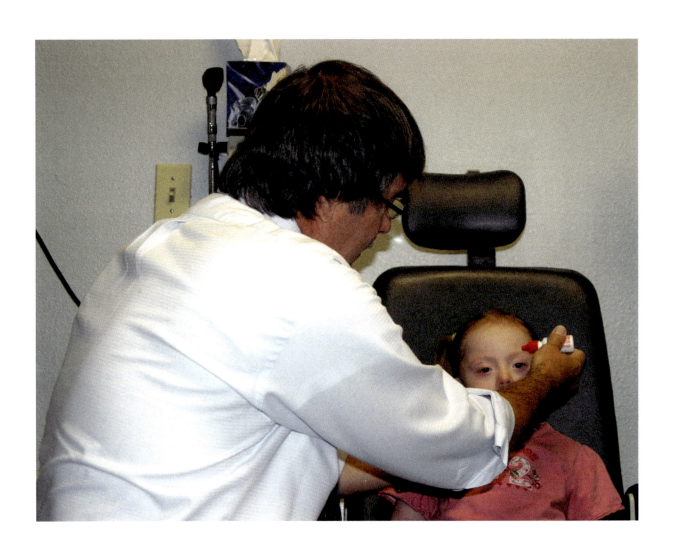

The Doctor put some drops in my eyes. He said it would take a little while for my eyes to dilate.

My mommy said he meant the black part of my eyes to get real big.

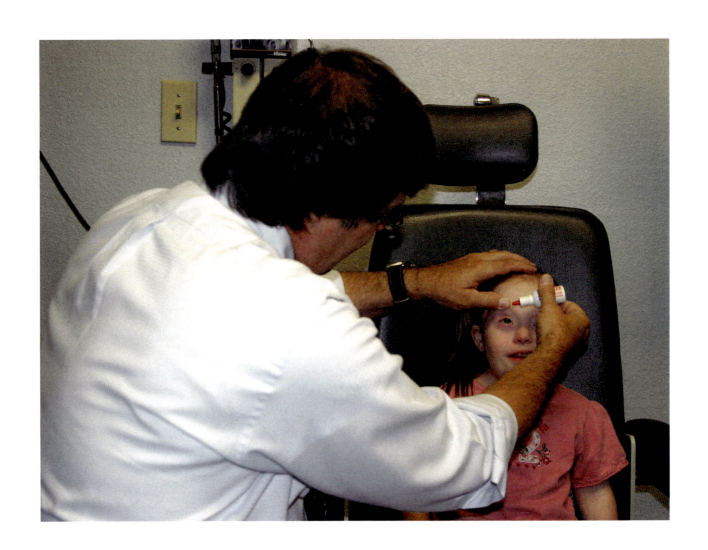

The doctor put drops in both of my eyes. It kind of tickled. I was having fun. I was a good girl. My mommy said so too.

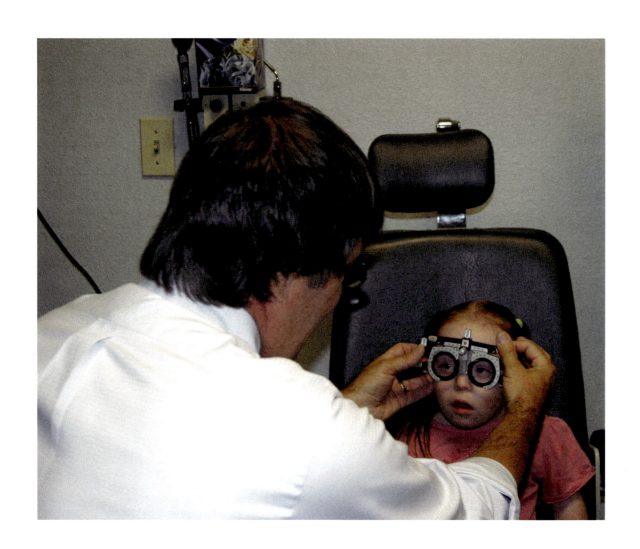

My doctor put some funny looking glasses on me too. He called them a *Trial Frame*. He put different lenses in them. I looked funny.

My doctor said the glasses were so he could test my eyes for refraction. My mommy said that means special glasses.

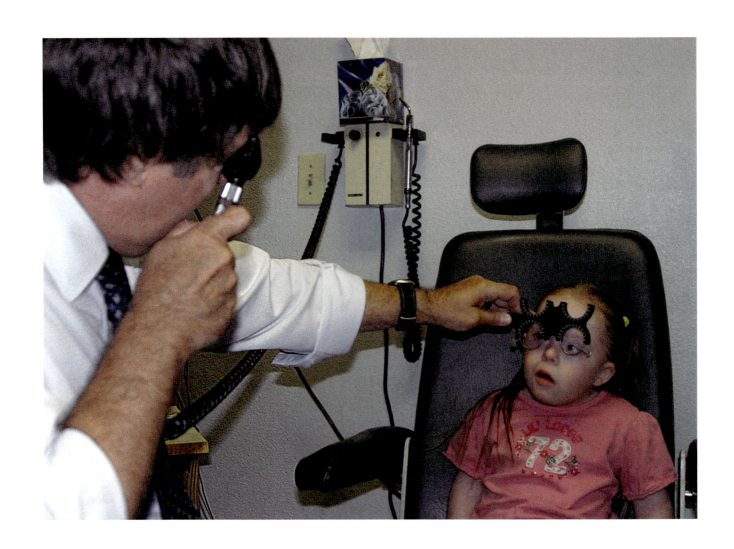

The doctor used another funny looking thing to look in my eyes. It was black and looked like a toy I have at home.

My mommy said it was a *Ophthalmoscope* and he used it for looking way deep into my eyes.

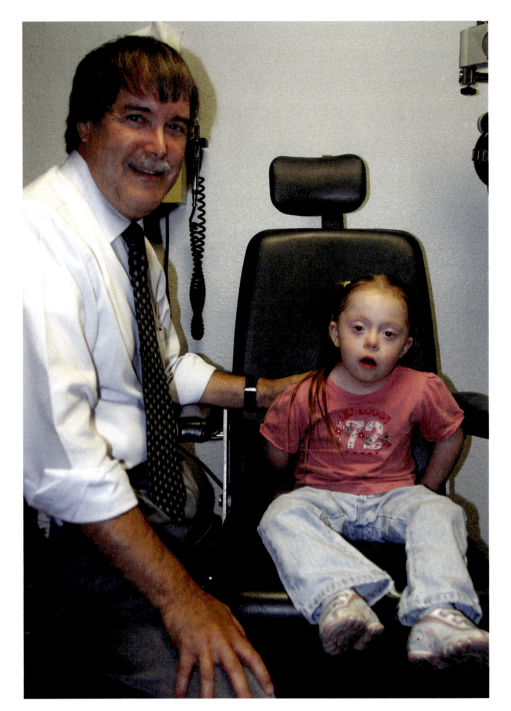

This is me with my doctor. His name is Dr. Kennedy. He is a nice person.

He told my mommy I have really special eyes and I need glasses.

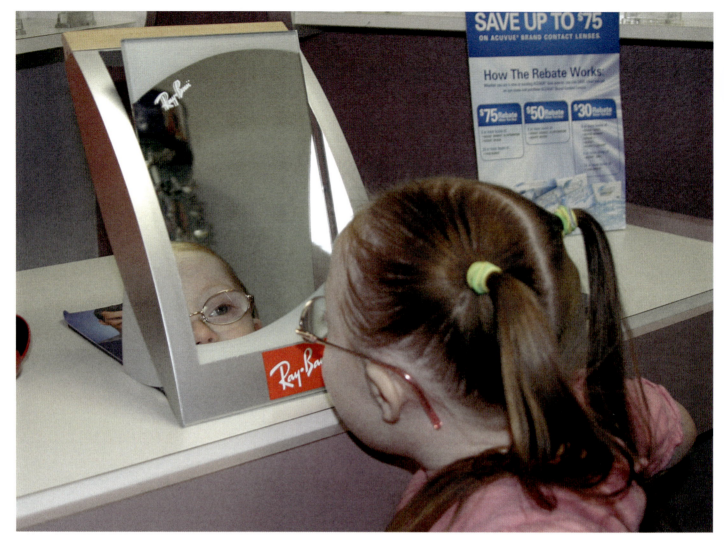

I tried on these glasses and I think they look good but I can't see myself in this mirror. I need a booster seat or something.

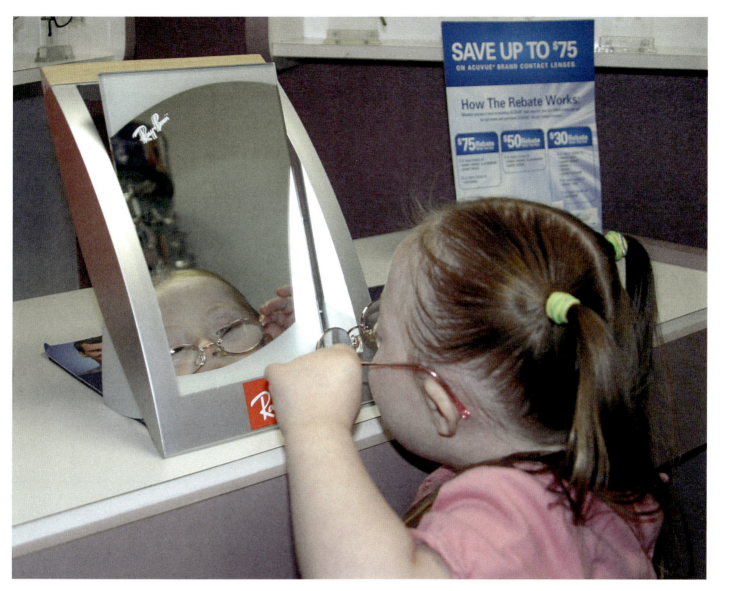

I like playing with these glasses. Do you think I look better with them on or off?

Melanie, the office lady, helped me pick out different glasses to try on. She showed me different ones I liked and did not like.

I like these glasses for wearing them outside. Do you think they fit my face?

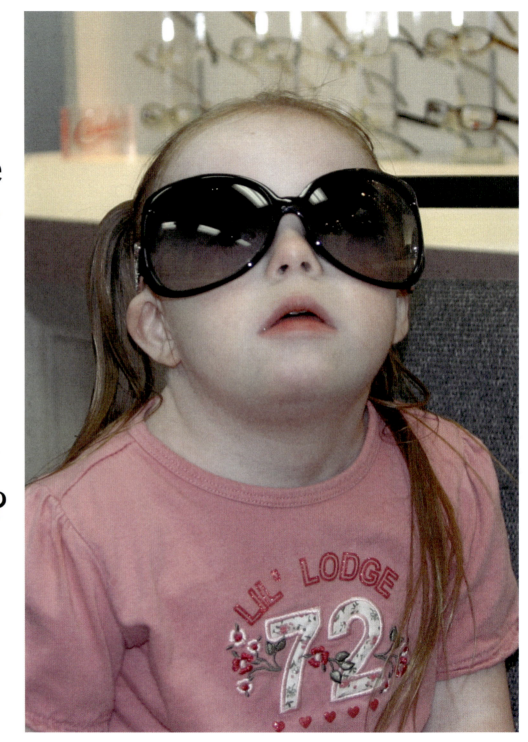

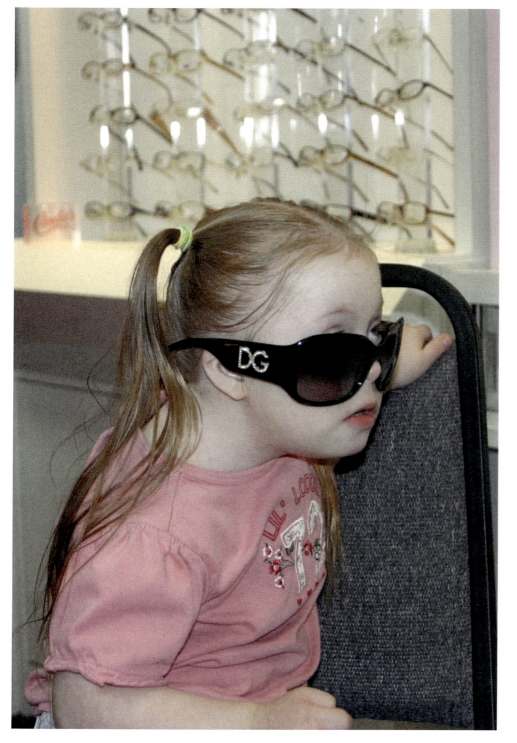

How do I look when I look over the glasses? I think they look cool. How about you?

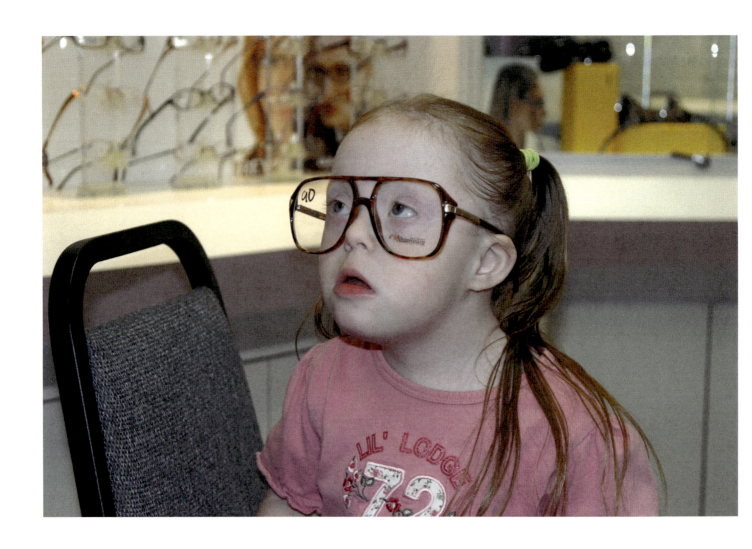

These glasses were fun to try on, but I want something different. I think these have to go back on the shelf.

My mommy said "no" to these too.

Melanie used a box thing to look into my eyes.

My mommy said it was a *Digital Pupilometer*. It is used to measure how far it is between my pupils. Pupils are black dots in our eyes.

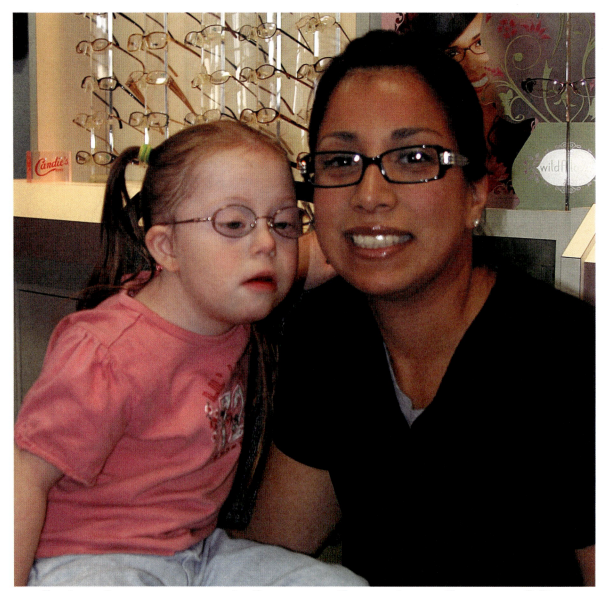

This is me with Melanie the office lady. She was very nice to me. She is my new friend.

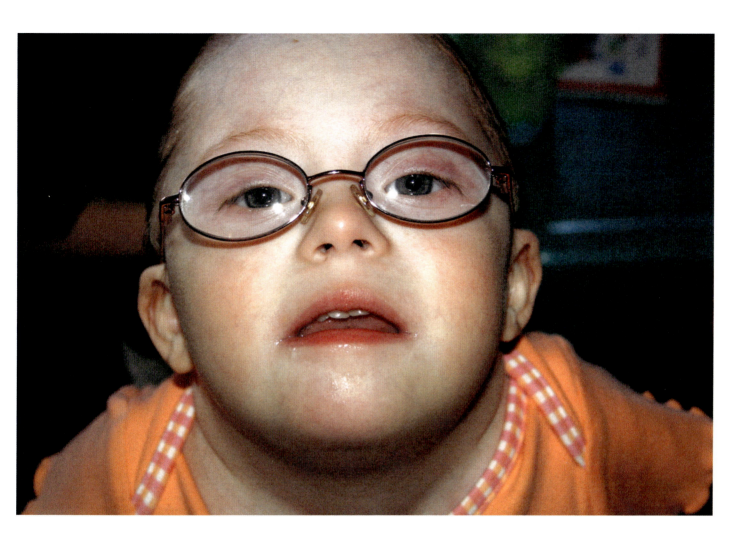

These are my new glasses. Do you think they fit?

When I go outside my new glasses get dark. It is like I have two new pairs of glasses!

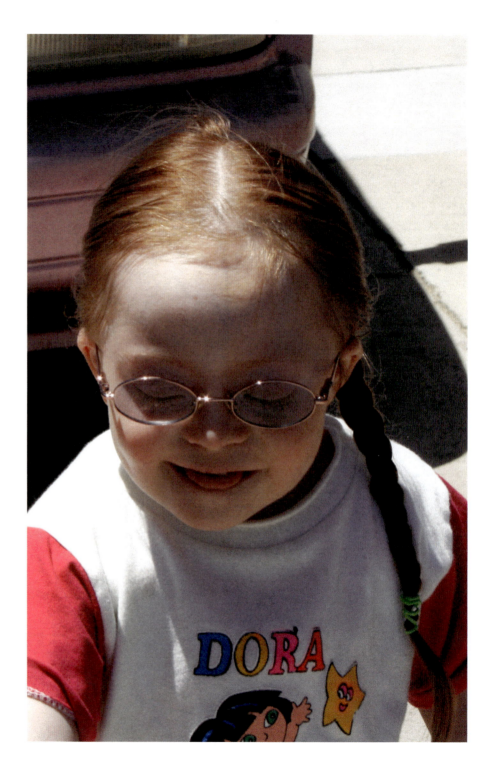

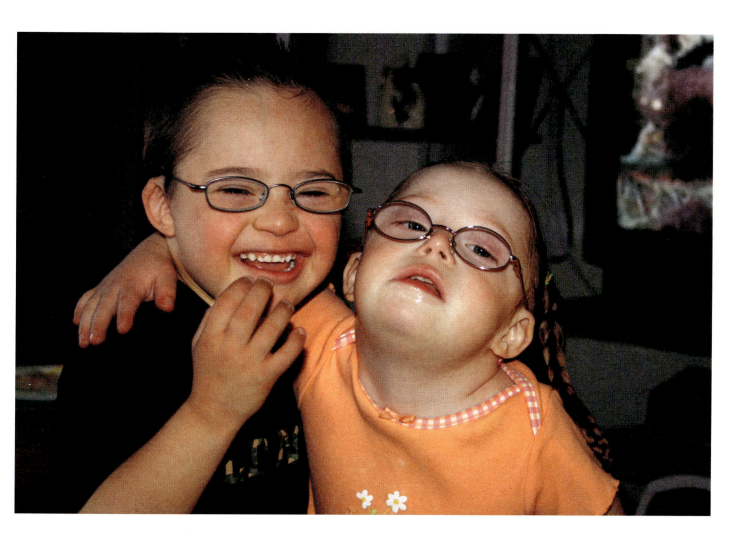

This is my best friend. His name is Andrew. He just got his glasses too.

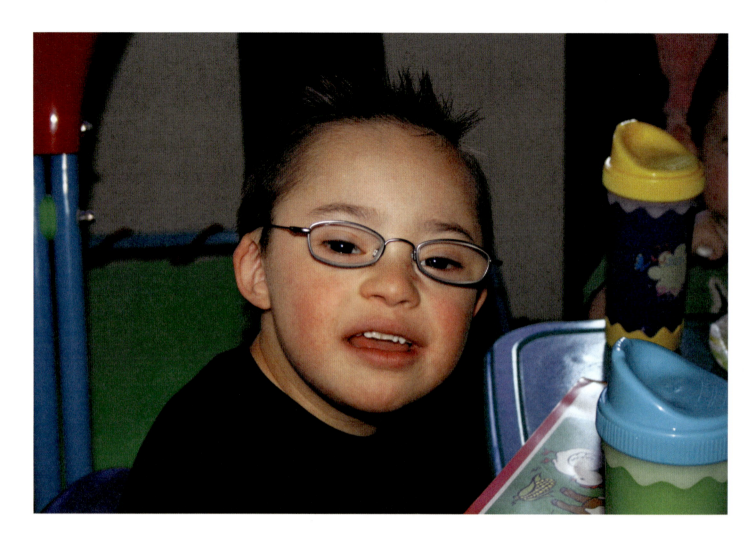

Doesn't Andrew look good in his new glasses?

Now that Andrew has his new glasses he can see too. He can read to his brother Cristian now.

Look for more of Tori's Adventures

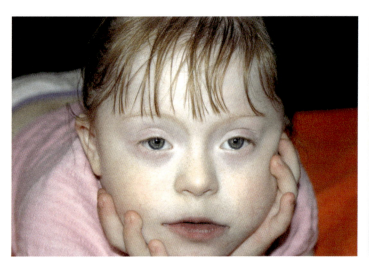

Made in the USA
Monee, IL
22 November 2019